The
Problem
Story

"It's not that I'm so smart, it's just that I stay with problems longer."

-Albert Einstein

The Problem Story

A Guide for Finding Solutions

M.B.Galenzavier
Illustrations by Natalie Galenzavier

THREE-SIXTY
PUBLICATIONS

www.three-sixty.com

THE PROBLEM STORY
by M.B. Galenzavier

Contact information:

Suite #235 440-10816 Macleod Trail SE

Calgary, AB T2J 5N8 Canada

theproblemstory.com / three-sixty.com

Book illustrations by Natalie Galenzavier

ISBN: 978-1-7751074-0-8

First Edition: August 2018

Dedicated to Natalie

To the love of my life – for your
infinite wisdom, encouragement, and affection.

Contents

Summary

Discussion Guide

IV | GALENZAVIER

Preface

THE EVIDENCE FOR PROBLEM -Solving Therapy (PST) and its effectiveness is well-documented. According to the American Psychological Association's (APA) Society of Clinical Psychology, PST has been shown to assist with issues such as major depression, generalized anxiety, emotional distress, relationship difficulties, and can even help mitigate the risk of self-harming behaviours ("APA Presidential Task Force on Evidence-Based Practice", 2006).

The APA reports that PST effectively addresses a variety of life problems - big and small. Problems like:

> [...] getting a divorce, experiencing the death of a loved one, losing a job, or having a chronic medical illness like cancer or heart disease. [...] the accumulation of multiple 'minor' occurrences, such as ongoing family problems, financial difficulties, constantly dealing with traffic jams, or tense relationships with co-workers or a boss. [...] [and] complex problems, such as 'wanting to find one's personal meaning of life.' ("What is PST?", APA, n.d.)

In 1971, researchers Thomas D'Zurilla and Marvin Goldfried laid the groundwork for PST with their "Social Problem-Solving Theory", and now for over 45 years, PST's benefits have been demonstrated in peer-reviewed studies from around the world; from treating emotional symptoms in family physician offices in the Netherlands (Hassink-Franke et al., 2011), to aiding low income/disadvantaged groups in South Africa (Van't Hof et al., 2011), to managing chronic disease in Iran (Azkhosh et al., 2014). However, despite these well-supported and cross-cultural findings, PST is still an approach that is yet to be brought into public discourse as a practical solution to many of life's difficulties.

The challenge in writing this book is twofold: 1) to take an evidence-based and largely under-represented methodology like PST and make it *approachable*, and 2) to take PST concepts and make them *applicable* to everyday life problems.

Whether readers are individuals engaged in counselling, managers struggling at work, or parents navigating their child's development - this is a story for everyone.

Many readers remember the fairy tales and fables of Grimm and Aesop - stories that use memorable animal characters to weave simple tales punctuated by dramatic morals and lessons. In this way, *The Problem Story* seeks to appeal to the reader's inner youth and tap into an old and familiar way of learning new information - through the power of story.

The techniques and theories highlighted in this story are derived directly from PST. As an evidence-based approach to managing life's problems, the PST skills and tools presented in this book may be the answer readers have been looking for. Readers are encouraged to review the *References + Recommended Resources* section on page 85 for further insight into PST and some of the techniques demonstrated in this book.

In the end, whether this book offers "the answer" or not, the key is to never stop exploring new ways of doing things - to never stop searching for solutions.

Introduction

PROBLEMS ARE A REALITY in life. In general, we humans are overwhelmingly resilient as we face problems in various forms each and every day. Yet, most of us approach the same problems in different ways and with varying degrees of success.

According to research (see pages 85-93), the way we perceive problems and address problems (problem solving) predicts how quickly we recover from problems, how severe our problems will be, and how deeply our problems will impact us.

This is all to say: If we never learned how to problem-solve in healthy and effective ways, then we could be doomed to repeat the same problems, exacerbate small problems, and experience unmanageable problems in multiple areas of life.

What's the good news? Problem-solving is a skill that can be learned just like any other. Much of problem-solving is about stopping and taking a step back, thinking things through, testing solutions, and making observations in step-by-step stages. That's it - that's problem-solving.

Once we learn a new and effective way of solving problems, we are equipped to approach *any* problem in life with the same set of tools and skills, regardless of the obstacle.

In reality, a problem is anything in need of a solution. Money troubles, ill health, stressful relationships, poor job performance - all problems needing solutions. The skills and tools taught in this story are meant to be applied to an assortment of scenarios.

On page 77, you'll find the *3-Step Solution Guide*, which offers a practical template for identifying and testing solutions to any problem. Lastly, an abridged version of this story can be found on page 51 (useful for those in a hurry or needing a recap of the story's major points).

Any problem can have its best possible solution realized with careful exploration and a commitment to experimentation. I hope you find what you're looking for in the story of Ms. Opossum, Mr. Badger, and Ms. Fox. *-M.B.G.*

The Story

— moral no.1 —

"A problem met with good problem -solving is less problematic."

IN A BEAUTIFUL GARDEN LIVED three unique creatures - Ms. Opossum, Mr. Badger, and Ms. Fox. Each of the animals saw the world in their own way and each had their own way of living in the world.

Ms. Opossum was a withdrawn creature, who was never interested in addressing life's challenges head-on. Ms. Opossum was peaceable, but would ignore and pretend to not see important details - often to her own detriment.

Ms. Opossum lacked the will to action and tended to address matters indirectly. While this approach had proven useful in getting out of a spot of trouble, "playing dead" to survive also meant Ms. Opossum lived an otherwise passive and avoidant way of life.

By contrast, Mr. Badger was a ferocious and intense creature. When faced with a problem, he wouldn't hesitate to dispatch it as quickly and as thoughtlessly as possible. His results were uneven, reckless, and sometimes disastrously harmful.

Mr. Badger lacked the patience to think things through, but possessed the ability to get things done. This useful survival mechanism helped him push through obstacles, but lead to an otherwise impulsive and close-minded way of life.

Last, but not least, was Ms. Fox. Always thinking, Ms. Fox had a rational and investigative mind. Intelligent yet humble, she would never call herself a genius, but knew enough to stop and reflect deeply and carefully when faced with a dilemma in life.

Ms. Fox realized that sometimes her first solution to a problem would not always work, and so, another solution must always be around the corner at the ready. She believed solutions needed to be tested again and again until a result was realized.

Ms. Fox possessed the will to problem-solve and persist - a useful and resilient survival skill that prepared her for any of the problems life threw her way.

Ms. Fox knew there were times when she would need to walk away like Ms. Opossum and times when she would have to fight like Mr. Badger. But more than anything, she knew that no single approach would guarantee a solution every time. Problem solving requires a combination of thought, flexibility, action, and tenacity.

"A problem met with good problem-solving is less problematic," thought Ms. Fox.

Go to page 58 for the discussion guide.

— moral no.2 —

"A problem for one is not always a problem for another."

NOW, THE GARDEN WHERE ALL OF the animals lived was full of bountiful food and fresh water - sustaining all varieties of species and natural life. Separated by a giant wall, the garden was divided into two equal sides.

The south-facing side of the garden, where Ms. Opossum, Mr. Badger, and Ms. Fox lived, received all of the warmth of the sun. Meanwhile, the north side of the wall stayed in the shade and remained darker, cooler, and wetter most of the season. The wall seemed to exist for no apparent reason and never bothered anyone in the garden - that is, except for Ms. Fox.

Seasons were getting hotter and Ms. Fox was growing more concerned about their resources. She suspected the wall would become a problem and worked very hard to convince all the animals that a solution for reaching the other side of the garden should be found. But try as she might, she simply could not make anyone see the problem she saw.

"A problem for one is not always a problem for another," thought Ms. Fox.

Go to page 60 for the discussion guide.

— moral no.3 —

"A problem is not a problem until it's a problem."

THE   SEPARATE   ARRANGEMENT
created by the wall pleased most every creature on
the south side. The radiant sun brought the growth
of food, warmth, and joy into the lives of each and
every animal.

However, it was during one particularly hot and dry season that the south side of the garden became warmer than it had ever been before.

Soon, the plant and animal life dwindled and Ms. Opossum, Mr. Badger, and Ms. Fox found themselves without food, and in some cases, without water.

Knowing the north side of garden was cooler and lusher created a new dilemma. The creatures wondered, "How do we get to the other side?". And for the first time, all of the animals in the garden saw the big wall as an obvious problem.

"A problem is not a problem until it's a problem," thought Ms. Fox.

Go to page 62 for the discussion guide.

— moral no.4 —

" A problem
avoided
makes for
unavoidable
new problems. "

FIRST UP WAS MS. OPOSSUM AND HER attempt to get over the wall. She walked up, took a good look at the long, towering structure and decided not to try.

Ms. Opossum began telling herself that it would be impossible to get over the wall; she told herself it wasn't important to try. She became so unmotivated to face the problem, she convinced herself that, in fact, there was no problem at all - the wall was never *really* an issue to begin with.

Ms. Opossum concluded that the problem of the wall - if there ever was one - must be someone else's issue. She walked away secretly perplexed, hungry, and unsure of what do next.

Ms. Opossum's solution was to avoid and deny the problem of the wall, which created two new problems: confusion and hunger.

"A problem avoided makes for unavoidable new problems," thought Ms. Fox.

Go to page 64 for the discussion guide.

— moral no.5 —

"A problem is always a problem when alternatives are neglected."

THEN ALONG CAME MR. BADGER.
He wasn't going to let some wall get in his way,
he determined. And with that, he began pumping
himself up for an attack.

With ferocity and gusto, Mr. Badger began
kicking-up debris, attacking the face of the wall
with his claws, gnawing at the cracks of the wall

with his fangs, and ramming the foot of the wall with his body.

Without a budge, the wall remained completely intact. Mr. Badger was exhausted and infuriated. In his tired and weary state, he declared that getting over the wall was impossible. Angered by this, he began lashing out at every little thing that remotely reminded him of the wall.

By ignoring other options and jumping to conclusions, Mr. Badger became erratic, blaming, burnt-out, and bitter.

"A problem is always a problem when alternatives are neglected," thought Ms. Fox.

Go to page 66 for the discussion guide.

— moral no.6 —

"A problem is often comprised of smaller, more solvable problems."

FINALLY THERE WAS MS. FOX. SHE
had been thinking long and hard about the wall
problem - far longer than any of the others had, in
fact. But still, Ms. Fox was no closer to a solution
than anyone else.

Ms. Fox took a stick and began scribbling in the dirt a list of all of the possible solutions she could think of. And after weighing the pros and cons of each item on her solution list, she selected three ideas which looked rather promising.

Idea number one: explore the wall for an opening. Ms. Fox began running along the wall hoping she might find where it ends or opens. But it seemed that the wall spanned endlessly.

Idea number two: dig under the wall. She dug until she struck the thick and tough clay of the earth - unable to dig any further. So far, no luck. But she still had one more idea to try.

"A problem is often comprised of smaller, more solvable problems," thought Ms. Fox.

Go to page 68 for the discussion guide.

— moral no.7 —

"A problem that's persistent is a problem in need of persistence."

NOW BY THIS POINT, MS. FOX HAD to take a moment, as she was feeling a touch disheartened. She knew facing this problem wouldn't be easy and that it would take both work and commitment, but she was having trouble keeping her spirits up.

Ms. Fox decided to talk to others about it and she was reminded of the all motivating factors for why she was seeking a solution - her desires, reasons, needs, and commitments. She desired freedom and the reasons were clear: she needed food, needed water, and she was committed to fight, committed to survive. It was all so important to her that she knew - even if some of her solutions failed - she had to keep going.

With this in mind, Ms. Fox began exploring idea number three in detail. This one was tricky, but had good potential. If she couldn't go through the wall, around the wall, or under the wall, then she must go over the wall! Ms. Fox needed a detailed plan. How would she get over the top of the wall? With her handy stick, she began scribbling and breaking-down idea number three into steps.

Finally, she concluded her plan. Tomorrow she would find the biggest tree with the longest branches in all of the garden, climb it, and then leap over the wall. In fact, Ms. Fox remembered seeing a massive oak tree as she ran the length of the wall in search of an opening.

Ms. Fox had a moment of doubt. Would the tree be close enough to the wall and could she jump far enough to make the gap? She would have to try. It was her best option.

At least something good may have come from her failed attempt at idea number one.

"A problem that's persistent is a problem in need of persistence," thought Ms. Fox.

Go to page 70 for the discussion guide.

— moral no.8 —

"A problem in the mind of others is a problem not easily remedied."

AS SOON AS MS. FOX FINISHED HER
plan she ran to tell Ms. Opossum and Mr. Badger.
Ms. Opossum was still forlorn and now completely
uninterested in any talk of the wall. The wall was
not her problem, she had surmised.

Likewise, when Mr. Badger was approached he was equally as dismissive. Angrily, he told Ms. Fox that he had already tried everything imaginable - throwing things at the wall, biting the wall, scratching the wall - and that no solution was possible.

Try as she might, Ms. Fox could not help the others arrive at the same conclusion to the problem - they simply didn't see the solution she saw.

"A problem in the mind of others is a problem not easily remedied," thought Ms. Fox.

Go to page 72 for the discussion guide.

— moral no.9 —

"A problem solved is not always a problem that stays solved."

THE FOLLOWING DAY MS. FOX knew exactly what she had to do - she found the ancient tree, leapt onto its great trunk, and scrambled across its wide-spanning branches. Ms. Fox inhaled a deep breath, took a good look at the other side, and caught glimpse of a pristine pond.

Quickly, she ran across the longest branch and leapt over the wall, plunging into the depths of the cool waters. In an instant, Ms. Fox swiftly paddled to shore. She could hardly believe she made it!

Suddenly, Ms. Fox was surrounded by all varieties of flourishing life, cool shade, and water. She ran with joy, stopping only to sate her hunger and quench her thirst.

But then suddenly she paused: There were no great oaks near the wall on this side. When the time comes, how would she ever get back to the south side? She pondered, "A problem solved is not always a problem that stays solved." Then, after a moment or two, a second thought dawned on her. "Ah," said Ms. Fox, "It's simply another problem I'll be ready to solve". *THE END*

Go to page 74 for the discussion guide.

Summary

CHARACTER SUMMARY

THE PASSIVE + AVOIDANT PROBLEM SOLVER	THE RATIONAL PROBLEM SOLVER	THE AGGRESSIVE + CARELESS PROBLEM SOLVER
—"plays dead"	—"thinks and thinks"	—"attacks everything!"
—ignores issues	—considers all options	—won't think things throug
—displaces blame	—takes responsiblity	—lashes out and is flippa
—doesn't try	—keeps an open-mind	—is impatient and impetuot
—gives-up easily	—keeps trying + testing	—over-reacts and burns—c

STORY SUMMARY

Page #6

Story Summary: Three animals - a fox, opossum, and badger - live in a garden. Each sees the world and its problems differently.

Message: Not everyone handles problems the same way - some don't do anything, some act without thinking, and some are careful and thoughtful.

Moral #1: "A problem met with good problem-solving is less problematic."

Page #16

Story Summary: The garden is divided north/south by a wall. The fox believes the wall is a problem, but cannot convince the others of what she sees.

Message: We cannot force others to believe a problem exists if they simply do not see it.

Moral #2: "A problem for one is not always a problem for another."

Page #20

Story Summary: One season, the south side of the garden becomes too warm. The problem is now all too evident. How can the animals get over the wall to the cooler, northern side of the garden?

Message: Identifying and defining a problem is the first step towards finding a solution.

Moral #3: "A problem is not a problem until it's a problem."

Page #24

Story Summary: The opossum approaches the problem of the wall, but gives up before trying - deciding it's impossible to solve.

Message: Avoiding or ignoring problems is a tempting, but temporary, solution.

Moral #4: "A problem avoided makes for unavoidable new problems."

Page #28

Story Summary: The badger attacks the wall. He is too impulsive and aggressive, and by ignoring other options, he burns-out and gives-up easily.

Message: Aggressively attacking a problem without thinking creates its own problems and hinders the search for solutions.

Moral #5: "A problem is always a problem when alternatives are neglected."

Page #32

Story Summary: The fox stops and thinks. She brainstorms a list of possible solutions to the problem. After weighing each idea, she begins testing.

Message: Analyze and break problems down into smaller pieces. Try solutions one-by-one.

Moral #6: "A problem is often comprised of smaller, more solvable problems."

Page #36

Story Summary: The fox tests many ideas, but she is disheartened by the lack of results. She decides to talk to others and is ultimately reminded of her motivations. She has one last idea to try.

Message: Don't give up! Talk to others and search for your inner motivation. Try, try, try! Keep trying solutions - even if some fail.

Moral #7: "A problem that's persistent is a problem in need of persistence."

Page #40

Story Summary: The fox believes she has found a solution, but cannot convince the opossum or the badger.

Message: We cannot force solutions on others - solutions must "make sense" on an individual level.

Moral #8: "A problem in the mind of others is a problem not easily remedied."

Page #44

Story Summary: Exercising her final and most promising idea, the fox climbs a large tree and in one daring leap she successfully launches over the top of the wall. Once on the north side of the wall, she realizes there are no trees near enough to leap back to the south side. How will she get back over the wall again? Without hesitation, the fox declares that it's just another problem she's ready to solve.

Message: Problems do not go away in life - there's always another one around the bend. We must be prepared with useful problem-solving skills.

Moral #9: "A problem solved is not always a problem that stays solved."

Discussion

Guide

DISCUSSION I

Moral #1: "A problem met with good problem-solving is less problematic."

- Problems exist. Life would not be possible without them. But we do not always approach problems in the most practical and reasonable ways.

- Sometimes we're avoidant like Ms. Opossum - ignoring problems, procrastinating, shifting responsibility, blaming others or circumstances.

- Other times we may be aggressive when solving problems, like Mr. Badger - reckless, careless, reactionary, thoughtless, and sloppy in our approach.

- But of course, we may also be like Ms. Fox - careful, rational, thoughtful, organized, and systematic when seeking out solutions.

- It should be emphasized that we don't always use *one way* of approaching problems - our problem orientation can shift depending on the issue. We may be more "badger" in our business affairs, but more "opossum" in our personal lives.

- This isn't to say we don't rely on one approach more often than others. We could ask ourselves: "How do I tend to approach problems? What style do I lean towards the most often? Do I avoid (opossum), over-react (badger), or do I define the problem and then measure out my options (fox)?".

- Can you think of examples of people in your life who are more "opossum", "badger", or "fox"?

DISCUSSION II

Moral #2: "A problem for one is not always a problem for another."

- Problems can be subjective. One person might see a problem, where another may not. Moreover, if someone doesn't see a problem themselves, it's no one else's responsibility to "change their mind" for them - it's just not realistic. We simply cannot change the beliefs of others this way (and we'll burn out trying).

- At most, we can share our observations, concerns, and ideas in hopes that others see our perspective. But alas, we must eventually let go, because we can never make others see a problem that's invisible to them. No one could be convinced that the wall was a problem - it would have to become an obvious problem for them before they would do anything.

- Therefore, it is safe to assume the first step to "finding a solution" in problem-solving is identifying and acknowledging that there is a problem. This was Ms. Fox's first step. Ms. Fox then tried to share her observations, but no one was interested in finding a solution. And understandably so. After all, why would anyone search for a solution to a problem they don't believe exists?

DISCUSSION III

Moral #3: "A problem is not a problem until it's a problem."

- What is a "problem"? How do we define what a problem is? When did the wall become a problem? The answer is when it became an obstacle that prevented the creatures in the garden from getting and doing what they needed to do to survive.

- A helpful but general definition of when something becomes a problem is when it begins interfering with our "normal" everyday functioning. If we are unable to do the things that are important or essential to us, we have an issue. Again, how we define our problems is important for when it comes time to search for solutions.

- Sometimes problems have been in front of us the entire time, we just never noticed them because they never really bothered us before. We all live with and encounter so-called "problems" which never prevent us from experiencing life or getting our work done, and so, the "problem" isn't a problem (until the day it maybe becomes a "real" problem). Like the wall in the story - just sitting there doing nothing. Sometimes the question is: Is the problem *enough* of a problem for you to want to solve it?

DISCUSSION IV

Moral #4: "A problem avoided makes for unavoidable new problems."

- It can take a lot of work to find a solution to a problem. It can sometimes feel like problem-solving is more trouble than it's worth. It may even seem like problem-solving creates a new kind of problem: the problem of more effort and more stress searching for a solution.

- So in other words, finding solutions take time, energy, and work. For the opossum in us, this deters us and makes us want to give up or pretend the problem doesn't exist. This is normal. Avoiding a problem (which is a problem in and of itself) is in fact a type of solution.

- However, avoidance is a temporary solution. Sure, we don't have to use any time or energy, but the original problem (the wall) hasn't gone away. Avoidance will always be a tempting option because it is so easy and works so well - for a while, at least. And that's why, one might say, there's a little "opossum" in us all.

DISCUSSION V

Moral #5: "A problem is always a problem when

alternatives are neglected."

- Simply put, problems are not enjoyable things. Much like pain, it's only natural to want to be relieved of a problem as quickly as possible. But when it comes to problem-solving, it's important not to confuse thinking quickly with thinking effectively.

- Too much too quickly, without first thinking, does not always lead to results (as seen with Mr. Badger). A rushed solution means a) we risk being ineffective, b) we risk making the problem worse or c) we risk creating a new problem. We'll waste even more time and energy correcting the mistakes we made from our hasty solution.

- The misdirected energy of aggressive and careless problem-solving can also take an emotional toll. It can lead to frustration and tension when our quick solutions or dismissals don't give us the results we're expecting. This approach can also seem thoughtless, which may alienate others. In the end, a badger-like approach can leave us feeling alone, drained, burnt-out, and ready to give-up problem-solving altogether.

DISCUSSION VI

Moral #6: "A problem is often comprised of smaller,
more solvable problems"

- Sometimes it feels like big problems require big solutions, however, this can overwhelm us. We can have a hard time seeing things in smaller pieces. Instead, we fixate on the larger chunk before us. But problems are often made-up of smaller problems - some that are easier to solve, some that are more difficult.

- When faced with a big problem we sometimes think we have no viable solutions (i.e., no idea what to do) and/or we have too many solutions (i.e., no idea where to begin). There's a three step response to this conundrum: 1) do a quick brainstorm for all possible solutions that appeal to you,

2) prioritize your top three most viable/realistic solutions, and finally, 3) begin testing your top three solutions one-by-one.

- This is what Ms. Fox does. First, she brainstorms all of her ideas without holding back, then she begins selecting her "top" solutions and testing them systematically. The goal here is to find something to try or something to do. When we feel defeated we tend to stop trying, and when we stop trying we tend to feel even more defeated. How do we break the cycle? Start testing solutions! Try a smaller part of the problem, try a smaller solution - try something.

DISCUSSION VII

Moral #7: "A problem that's persistent is a problem in need of persistence."

- Even with the "right" kind of thinking, the "right" kind of tools, and the "right" kind of support, some problems are not easily resolved. In fact, some problems will never have the kind of resolution or outcome we're hoping for. Understandably, the reality of this can leave us feeling disheartened and disillusioned.

- Problem-solving isn't always about getting the solution of our dreams, it's about exploring all of the available options and trying realistic solutions one-by-one until one sticks. But how do we keep our spirits up as we test - as we experience failure after failure in search of a solution?

- Ms. Fox reaches out, talks, and explores her own inner motivations. She reminds herself why she was searching for a solution in the first place. We need supportive people to bounce ideas off of and we need our own reminders of why we are doing the things that we are doing. These reminders do not come easily, but they are powerful. We have to keep asking ourselves important questions about what motivates us towards finding a solution - our desires, ability, reasons, needs, and commitment.

DISCUSSION VIII

Moral #8: "A problem in the mind of others is a problem not easily remedied."

- Remember Moral #2 - "A problem for one is not always a problem for another"? Remember how hard it is to convince others that there is a problem in the first place? Well, when it comes to changing the minds of others, offering solutions is just as tricky.

- Whenever we tell someone what they "should" do (i.e., offering them a solution that we think we've noticed), they're secretly sizing-up the suggestion (and you) while trying to figure out if it jives with their own beliefs about the problem. They're secretly wondering how practical the idea is, how useful, and/or how applicable it is to them. Think about your own experience. Have you ever been told to do something you didn't want to do - something you simply didn't believe was the solution?

- All this is not to say that we must give up trying to "help" others, or to show them our perspective on a problem. What it means is that we must know the limits and the boundaries of our influence over others. Finding a solution that works for us may not be a solution that works for others. All we can do is present the solutions we see as helpful or useful. Ultimately, we cannot change the minds of others, we can only attempt to better communicate our perspective.

DISCUSSION IX

Moral #9: "A problem solved is not always a problem that stays solved."

- Life is full of an assortment of problems in need of resolution. Some problems are harder, some are easier, but problems persist. This is to say: Problems are normal! How we respond to these problems is the key to our survival. Like Ms. Fox, we must be "rational problem solvers" - someone who stops and thinks through problems and solutions carefully.

- Part of being a realistic and rational problem solver is knowing that problems are a natural part of life, and that solutions (even the best thought-out ones) are not always the end of the story. In many ways, all of life is temporary - the good and the bad, the problems and the solutions. The end of one problem might be the start of another one. Coming to terms with this ebb and flow of life is central to being a true "problem solver".

- In the end, the key to sustainable problem-solving is learning skills which can be applied to a variety of problem scenarios. This way, when a new problem emerges, we're ready! Some of us go through life encountering problem after problem and instead of learning new ways of doing things, we fall into crisis after crisis. It is frustrating, exhausting, and a seemingly endless cycle. Ms. Fox's approach to problem solving is a demonstration of the techniques and skills that can make us all more resilient - ready for anything thrown our way.

3 - Step

Solution Guide

Step 1 : The Problem List

Things you'll need:

- Blank paper/writing instrument

- Timer/clock

- Self-awareness

a. Set your timer for 2 minutes.

b. Write a list of all of the problems you're experiencing right now. *Don't hold back!*

c. Narrow down and circle your "number one" most pressing problem (the one that you want to begin solving first). *If you can't decide, think of the problem you'd be most relieved to have gone today.*

MS. FOX'S EXAMPLE:

problem list

~~GARDEN IS TOO HOT~~

~~FOOD IS SCARCE~~

~~WATER IS DWINDLING~~

WALL IS BLOCKING LUSHER SIDE OF GARDEN

2mins

Step 2: The Solution List

Things you'll need:

- Your "number one problem" to work on

- Another blank piece of paper

- Timer/clock

- Creative thinking

a. With your "number one problem" in mind, set your timer for 2 minutes.

b. Brainstorm a list of *all* of the solutions you can think of. *In brainstorming, no idea is too unrealistic!*

c. Finally, begin weighing the pros and cons of each idea. Select your top three "most realistic" ideas (ideas you're confident you could try now).

MS. FOX'S EXAMPLE:

solution list

(2mins)

		+	-
②	DIG UNDER WALL	I'M GOOD AT DIGGING	LOTS OF WORK INVOLVED
①	RUN AROUND WALL/ FIND OPENING	MAYBE THE SIMPLEST SOLUTION	IT'S A VERY, VERY LONG WALL
③	GO OVER THE WALL	I'M AGILE AND GOOD AT JUMPING	THE WALL IS TALL AND I CAN'T CLIMB
	~~STAY PUT~~	~~WON'T HAVE TO~~ DO ANYTHING	~~MAY NOT SURVIVE!~~

Step 3: Solution Testing

Things you'll need:

- Your "top three solutions" to try

- Another blank piece of paper

- Open-mindedness

a. Pick a solution to test (the one that sounds the most appealing and realistic to you right now).

b. Identify your solution's "W5": *Who* will be involved in the solution? *What* will be done? *Where* and *when* specifically? Finally, *why* do you want this solution (i.e., your motivation)?

c. Observe! Did you get the results you wanted? If not, try again or go to the next solution on your list.

MS. FOX'S EXAMPLE:

solution testing

SOLUTION: GO OVER THE WALL

WHO: ME

WHAT: CLIMB A TREE, LEAP OVER WALL

WHERE: THE LARGE OAK TREE NEAREST TO THE WALL

WHEN: TOMORROW MORNING

WHY: BECAUSE I MUST SURVIVE!

References +

Recommended

Resources

REFERENCES

APA Literature

"APA Presidential Task Force on Evidence-Based
Practice" (2006). *Evidence-based practice in
psychology.* American Psychologist, 61,
271-285.

"What is Problem Solving Therapy?" (n.d.). Retrieved
from http:/www.div12.org/sites/default/files/
WhatIsProblemSolvingTherapy.pdf

Clinical Trials

Alexopoulos et al., (2011). "Problem-solving therapy
and supportive therapy in older adults with
major depression and executive dysfunction:
Effect on disability"

Azkhosh et al., (2014). "The Effectiveness of Problem-
Solving Therapy on Coping Skills in women
with type 2 diabetes"

Choi et al., (2014). "Six-month postintervention depression and disability outcomes of in-home telehealth problem-solving therapy for depressed, low-income, homebound older adults"

Dowrick et al., (2000). "Problem-solving treatment and group psychoeducation for depression: Multicentre randomised controlled trial"

Ell et al., (2008). "Randomized controlled trial of collaborative care management of depression among low-income patients with cancer"

Garand et al., (2013). "Effects of problem-solving therapy on mental health outcomes in family caregivers of persons with a new diagnosis of mild cognitive impairment or early dementia: A randomized controlled trial"

Harpole et al., (2005). "Improving depression out comes in older adults with comorbid medical illness"

Hassink-Franke et al., (2011). "Effectiveness of problem-solving treatment by general practice registrars for patients with emotional symptoms."

Hopko et al., (2013). "Behavioral activation and problem-solving therapy for depressed breast cancer patients: Preliminary support for decreased suicidal ideation"

Katon et al., (2004). "The Pathways Study: A randomized trial of collaborative care in patients with diabetes and depression"

Nezu (1986). "Efficacy of a social problem-solving therapy approach for unipolar depression"

Rivera et al., (2008). "Problem-solving training for family caregivers of persons with traumatic brain injuries: A randomized controlled trial"

Robinson et al., (2000). "Escitalopram and problem-solving therapy for prevention of poststroke depression: A randomized controlled trial"

Unützer et al., (2002). "Collaborative care management of late-life depression in the primary care setting: A randomized controlled trial"

Van't Hof et al., (2011). "The Effectiveness of Problem-Solving Therapy in Deprived South African Communities"

Meta-analyses and Systematic Reviews

Barth et al., (2013). "Comparative efficacy of seven psychotherapeutic interventions for patients with depression: A network meta-analysis."

Bell & D'Zurilla (2009). "Problem-solving therapy for
   depression: A meta-analysis"

Cape et al., (2010). "Brief psychological therapies for
   anxiety and depression in primary care: Meta-
   analysis and meta-regression."

Cuijpers, van Straten, & Warmerdam (2007).
   "Problem-solving therapies for depression: A
   meta-analysis"

Gellis & Kenaley (2008). "Problem-solving therapy
   for depression in adults: A systematic review."

Malouff, Thorsteinsson, & Schutte (2007).
   "The efficacy of problem-solving therapy in
   reducing mental and physical health
   problems: A meta-analysis"

Nieuwsma et al., (2012) "Brief psychotherapy for
   depression: A systematic review and meta-
   analysis"

RECOMMENDED RESOURCES

Books

Eskin (2012). *Problem-Solving Therapy in the Clinical Practice.*

Gellis & Nezu (2011). *Cognitive Behavior Therapy with Older Adults: Innovations Across Care Settings.* Chapter 13: "Depression treatment for homebound medically ill older adults: Using evidence-based problem-solving therapy"

Mynors-Wallis (2005). *Problem-Solving Treatment for Anxiety and Depression: A Practical Guide.*

Nezu, Nezu, & D'Zurilla (2012). *Problem-Solving Therapy: A Treatment Manual*

Nezu, Nezu, & Clark (2008). *Risk Factors in Depression.* Chapter 12: "Social problem-solving as a risk factor for depression"

Nezu, Nezu, & Clark (2006). *Solving Life's Problems: A 5-Step Guide to Enhanced Well-Being*

Web

Division 12 of the American Psychological Association (2013). "Problem-Solving Therapy for Depression". https://www.div12.org/psycho logical-treatments/disorders/depression/ problem-solving-therapy-for-depression/

US Dept. of Veterans Affairs & US Dept. of Defense (n.d.). "Moving Forward" [Free mobile app, interactive 6-hour web program]. https://itunes.apple.com/us/ app/moving-forward/id804300239?mt=8

University of Auckland, Dept. of Psychological Medicine (n.d.). "7-Steps of PST" [Videos]. http://www.problemsolvingtherapy.ac.nz/3. html

Washington University, Dept. of Psychiatry and

Behavioral Sciences (Oct. 16, 2008). *Webinar:*

Evidence-Based Depression Care Management:

Improving Mood-Promoting Access to

Collaborative Treatment (IMPACT). https://

www.ncoa.org/resources/webinar-

evidence-based-depression-care-management-

improving-mood-promoting-access-

to-collaborative-treatment-impact/

About the author

MATTHEW BRADY GALENZAVIER
is a social worker, educator, and author with a
breadth of experience working with vulnerable
populations in law enforcement, primary care,
and public health. His areas of special interest
intersect the fields of mental health, social and
behavioural health, and health promotion. He
is the co-founder of Three-Sixty Wellbeing, a
social enterprise dedicated to making health
and wellbeing resources more accessible
through innovative services, health promotion,
and education. He lives with his wife, Natalie
Galenzavier in Calgary, Alberta, Canada.

www.ingramcontent.com/pod-product-compliance
Lightning Source LLC
Chambersburg PA
CBHW072040040426
42447CB00012BB/2953